W9-AKU-118

Understanding the Elements of the Periodic Table™

MAGNESIUM

Edward Willett

12   24

Mg

rosen publishing's
rosen
central

New York

Published in 2007 by The Rosen Publishing Group, Inc.
29 East 21st Street, New York, NY 10010

Library of Congress Cataloging-in-Publication Data
Willett, Edward, 1959–
Magnesium / Edward Willett.
p. cm. —(Understanding the elements of the periodic table)
Includes bibliographical references and index.
ISBN-13: 978-1-4042-1007-3
ISBN-10: 1-4042-1007-5 (library binding)
1. Magnesium. 2. Periodic law—Tables. 3. Chemical elements. I. Title.
QD181.M4.W55 2007
546'.392—dc22
                                                          2006020732

Manufactured in the United States of America

On the cover: Magnesium's square on the periodic table of elements. Inset: The atomic structure of magnesium.

Contents

Introduction   4

Chapter One   Magnesium Is Everywhere   6

Chapter Two   Magnesium and
the Periodic Table   14

Chapter Three   How Magnesium Is Recovered 24

Chapter Four   Magnesium Compounds 30

Chapter Five   Magnesium and You 36

The Periodic Table of Elements   42

Glossary   44

For More Information   45

For Further Reading   46

Bibliography   46

Index   47

Introduction

In the summer of 1618, a terrible drought ravaged England. Man and beast needed every drop of water they could find, so it surprised Henry Wicker, a farmer near the town of Epsom in Surrey, to see a pool of water on Epsom Common being ignored by nearby cattle. Curious, Wicker tasted the water and found that it was very bitter. He took a sample of it and let it evaporate. The sample left behind crystals that soon became known as Epsom salts. Either Wicker or one of his neighbors—we don't really know who—discovered that soaking in the water relaxed sore muscles and softened rough skin. Someone also discovered that Epsom salts made an excellent laxative. Over the next few decades, the crystals became renowned across Europe as a treatment for all kinds of medical conditions, especially constipation.

Epsom salts are actually a compound of the element magnesium (Mg): magnesium sulfate heptahydrate ($MgSO_4 \cdot 7H_2O$). Most of the Epsom salts consumed in Europe didn't come from the town of Epsom at all, but were extracted from other briny water high in magnesium, including seawater.

Today, you can buy Epsom salts (which still don't come from Epsom). However, magnesium, identified as an element almost 140 years after Wicker's discovery and eventually isolated fifty years after that, has many more uses besides easing constipation.

Pure magnesium, like these slivers, is a silvery white metal. However, magnesium never occurs in its pure state in nature, but only as part of various compounds.

Magnesium oxide (MgO), also called magnesia, is made into heat-resistant bricks for furnaces and fireplaces, is added to fertilizers, and supplements cattle feed. Mixed with aluminum (Al) to form an alloy, magnesium is used in car bodies and aircraft fuselages. Added to molten iron (Fe) and steel, magnesium is used to remove sulfur (S). Bicycle frames, car wheels, power tools, lawn mowers, cameras, and more are made from the metal and its alloys.

Magnesium is crucial to all life on Earth. Humans need about 200 milligrams of it every day; fortunately, it's readily available in much of the food we eat. One reason is that magnesium is an essential part of the chlorophyll molecule. Chlorophyll, which makes plants green, captures the energy of the sun so plants can turn carbon dioxide and water into glucose, plants' basic food.

Magnesium has also been used to destroy life. During the Second World War (1939–1945), infernos ignited by up to 500,000 4.4-pound (2-kilogram) magnesium bombs dropped in less than an hour destroyed entire cities; magnesium, once it starts to burn, is almost impossible to extinguish. Harmless, deadly, and life-giving all at the same time, magnesium is a metal of contradictions.

Chapter One
Magnesium Is Everywhere

Although magnesium is not found in its pure elemental state in nature, it is not a rare element. In fact, it's about the seventh most abundant element in the earth's crust, making up between 2 and 3 percent of it by weight. If the mantle, the molten rock that lies under the crust, is taken into account, it's the third most abundant element on the earth, since the mantle is largely composed of olivine and pyroxene, magnesium-containing minerals. Furthermore, it's estimated that every cubic mile of ocean water contains 12 billion pounds (1.3 billion kilograms/cubic kilometers) of magnesium.

Magnesium is found naturally combined with other elements, in substances called compounds. Various compounds of magnesium have been used for centuries. But because magnesium doesn't exist in nature in its pure form, it wasn't recognized as an element until the eighteenth century. Pure magnesium wasn't isolated until the nineteenth century. That's because magnesium makes very stable compounds; that is, it is reactive toward making chemical bonds with other elements. These compounds are hard to break down, so it's difficult to separate out the magnesium they contain.

Magnesium sulfate ($MgSO_4$) or its hydrated (water-containing) form, magnesium sulfate heptahydrate ($MgSO_4 \bullet 7H_2O$), known as Epsom salt

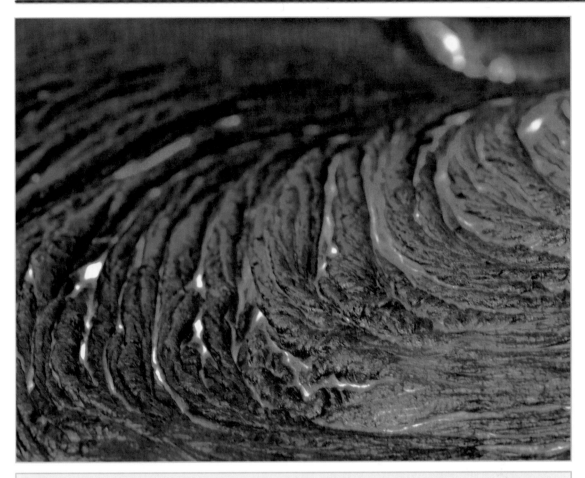

Pahoehoe lava flows from Kilauea Volcano, Hawaii. Pahoehoe lava is high in magnesium, calcium, and iron, and low in silica, sodium, and potassium.

or the mineral epsomite, is one such compound. Another is calcium magnesium carbonate [$CaMg(CO_3)_2$], better known as the mineral dolomite, which is used in construction (primarily as a decorative stone) and in the manufacturing of some cements. A third is sepiolite, or meerschaum [$Mg_4Si_6O_{15}(OH)_2 \bullet 6(H_2O)$]. This soft white mineral, so light it's sometimes found floating in the Black Sea, has been used for centuries in Turkey to make elaborate pipes for smoking tobacco. It's soft when first extracted from the earth and thus easily carved, but it hardens when dried by the sun or in a warm room, and it can then be carved and polished.

It's an Element!

Around 1750, chemist Joseph Black, while studying at the universities of Edinburgh and Glasgow in Scotland, began experimenting with another magnesium compound. Chemists of his day called it magnesia alba (from Italian, meaning "white magnesia"). Today, chemists refer to it as hydrated magnesium carbonate [$4MgCO_3 \bullet Mg(OH)_2 \bullet 4H_2O$]. Black discovered that when magnesia alba was heated, it gave off water and a gas. The gas had odd properties—for instance, if he poured it over a candle, the candle would go out. Black called the gas "fixed air." It is now known as carbon dioxide (CO_2).

Why Magnesium?

Besides *magnesia alba*, or "white magnesia," chemists in the eighteenth century knew of a substance they called *magnesia nigra*, or "black magnesia." Today, chemists call black magnesia manganese oxide (MnO_2).

Magnesia is a prefecture (state) in Greece in the region of Thessalia, where both magnesium and manganese (Mn) ores are abundant. The region is named after the Magnetes, members of a Macedonian tribe who lived there prior to 1300 BC. The Magnetes got their name from their supposed ancestor, the legendary Greek hero Magnes, son of the god Zeus and the mortal princess Thyia.

The words "magnet" and "magnetism" are also derived from "Magnesia," not because magnesium and manganese are magnetic (they aren't), but because magnetite, or lodestone, a naturally magnetized iron oxide, is found in the region.

In the course of his experiments, Black found that although heating calcium carbonate ($CaCO_3$) also produced carbon dioxide, the resulting residue, quicklime (calcium oxide [CaO]) was different from the residue produced by heating magnesia alba. This convinced him that magnesia alba contained a previously unrecognized element—that is, one of the basic substances that cannot be broken down into other substances by any amount of heat or force.

In 1792, Austrian chemist Anton Rupprecht heated magnesia with charcoal (one form of elemental carbon [C]) and managed to produce an impure form of metallic magnesium. He called the metal *austrium*. But credit for being the first to isolate pure magnesium goes to the English chemist Sir Humphry Davy. In 1808, he finally found a way to separate magnesium from the other elements to which it bound itself so tightly.

Davy Isolates Magnesium

Sir Humphry Davy had become interested in electrolysis. In electrolysis, a compound is melted or dissolved in a liquid solvent. Two electrodes are immersed in the fluid, and an electrical current is passed between them. One electrode, the cathode, is negatively charged, while the other, the anode, is positively charged. Ions are atoms that have either lost or gained an electron, giving them an electrical charge. When an ionic compound—a compound that is made up of ions—is dissolved or melted, the ions that make up the compound can move about more freely than in a solid. Positively charged ions are attracted to the cathode, while negatively charged ions are attracted to the anode. Once they reach the electrodes, the ions either give up (at the anode) or gain (at the cathode) electrons. As a result, the different ions that make up the compound slowly but continuously gather at each electrode.

Davy had already found that by passing electricity through water, he could break it down into hydrogen (H) and oxygen (O), in the form of the

Sir Humphry Davy isolated pure magnesium for the first time in 1808 via electrolysis, using equipment similar to that being used in this re-enactment of his experiment. Earlier, he had used electrolysis to isolate potassium and sodium.

molecules H_2 and O_2, respectively. When he tried passing a current through solid potash (an impure form of potassium carbonate, K_2CO_3), dampened so it would carry electricity, he was able to isolate potassium (K) metal.

With further modification of his process, he was able to isolate small quantities of magnesium. To produce magnesium, he mixed moistened magnesium oxide—magnesia—with the mercury-bearing compound mercuric oxide (HgO). He placed the resulting mud or paste on a platinum (Pt) plate, which was used as the anode.

Next, Davy made a small hollow in the paste into which he put a drop of mercury (Hg) and covered everything with a naphtha (a flammable liquid hydrocarbon mixture similar to gasoline). Finally, he connected the platinum plate and the drop of mercury to the battery with wires. An amalgam (mixture) of mercury and magnesium formed where the electrode entered the drop of mercury. He transferred that amalgam to a glass tube and heated it to drive off the mercury, leaving behind the pure magnesium.

Davy described the element as a white, lustrous solid. He wanted to call the new metal magnium, so that it wouldn't be confused with manganese, but the name magnesium stuck instead.

More details about magnesium's properties were recorded by the French scientist Antoine-Alexandre-Brutus Bussy, who heated magnesium chloride ($MgCl_2$) and potassium together in a glass tube in 1831, producing potassium chloride and a significant amount of pure magnesium.

Properties of Magnesium

Magnesium is a silvery-white metal. It's very light. The density (the mass of a given volume of a substance) of magnesium is only 1.74 grams per cubic centimeter, compared to aluminum's (Al) 2.7 grams per cubic centimeter and iron's 7.87 grams per cubic centimeter.

Although it's very hard to set fire to a large mass of magnesium, fine slivers or particles of magnesium catch fire readily and burn with a brilliant white light.

It's not easy to extinguish burning magnesium, since unlike most substances, it can burn not only in oxygen (combining with the oxygen to form magnesium oxide), but also in nitrogen (the element N, which occurs as N_2), which it combines with to form magnesium nitride (Mg_3N_2) and carbon dioxide (CO_2), producing magnesium oxide and carbon (C).

It combines with oxygen so readily that dousing burning magnesium with water (H_2O) can actually intensify the fire: the magnesium

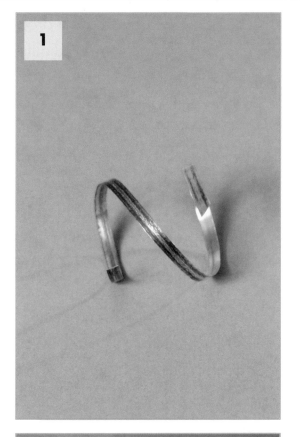

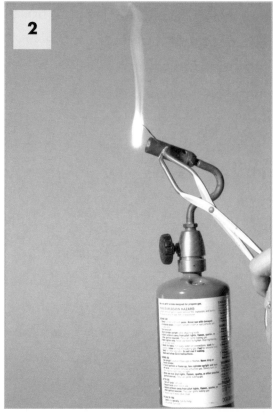

A fine ribbon of magnesium (photo 1) ignites easily (photo 2) and burns with a brilliant white light (photo 3). Once burning, magnesium is almost impossible to extinguish.

Flash!

Beginning in the 1860s, photographers burned magnesium ribbon to provide a bright light for taking photographs in the dark. Within a few years, photographers began experimenting with using powdered magnesium, which provided shorter flashes of light. In the mid-1880s, the use of flash powder became widespread. Flash powder consisted of magnesium powder mixed (usually) with potassium perchlorate ($KClO_4$), which served as an additional source of oxygen to enhance combustion.

Camera flash bulbs like this one had filaments of magnesium, ignited by an electrical charge.

In the 1930s, the first commercially available flash bulbs appeared. These glass bulbs contained slender threads of magnesium ignited by an electrical charge when a photo was taken. (Afterward, the bulbs were too hot to handle.) Magnesium powder is still used in fireworks to provide brilliant white sparks, and in warning and signaling flares, again because it burns with such a brilliant white light.

strips the oxygen out of the water, producing hydrogen gas (H_2), which makes the fire burn even hotter.

Inert gases such as helium (H) or argon (Ar) will extinguish burning magnesium. More typically, burning magnesium in the form of small chips or shavings is smothered with a dry chemical extinguisher [e.g., graphite and dry sodium chloride (NaCl)].

Chapter Two
Magnesium and the Periodic Table

agnesium's ability to form very stable compounds is the result of its atomic makeup. The ancient Greeks came up with both the concept of the atom and the concept of the elements. They believed atoms were the smallest particles into which matter could be subdivided. They also believed that everything was made up of a mixture of just four elements: earth, air, fire, and water.

Eventually the concept of the atom and the concept of elements came together, and scientists realized that each element was made up of unique atoms. An atom, in other words, is the smallest particle into which an element can be subdivided and still be identified as that specific element.

But an understanding of the elements, and what gave each its unique characteristics, didn't really arise until scientists determined that atoms themselves were made up of smaller, subatomic particles called protons, neutrons, and electrons.

Protons have a positive electrical charge, electrons have a negative electrical charge, and neutrons have no charge. Each atom consists of a nucleus at the center of the atom that is made up of protons and neutrons (except for most hydrogen atoms, which have only a single proton as a nucleus and no neutrons at all). The electrons surround the nucleus in a series of interpenetrating layers, or shells, each of which can hold only a certain number of electrons. The shell closest to the nucleus, for example,

The most common form of magnesium has twelve protons and twelve neutrons in its nucleus (some are hidden in this view), and twelve electrons in three electron shells.

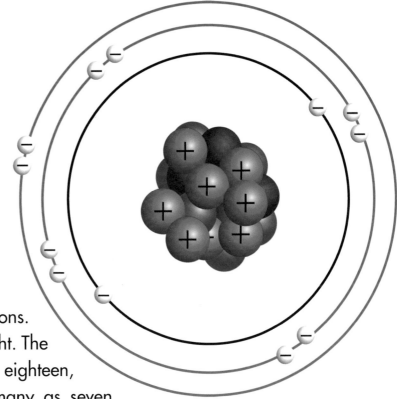

can hold only two electrons. The next shell can hold eight. The third shell can hold up to eighteen, and so on, through as many as seven shells to form all the known elements. Elemental magnesium has twelve protons in its nucleus and twelve electrons in its electron shells.

Most of the naturally occurring magnesium atoms have twelve neutrons in their nuclei. While the number of electrons and the number of protons are always the same in a neutral atom of an element, the number of neutrons can vary. Atoms of an element with differing numbers of neutrons are called isotopes. The isotopes of an element are identified by a number that totals the protons and neutrons in the nucleus (called the mass number).

Magnesium has three naturally occurring isotopes. Magnesium-24, with twelve neutrons, makes up 79 percent of the world's magnesium; magnesium-25, with thirteen neutrons, occurs 10 percent of the time; and magnesium-26, with fourteen neutrons, occurs 11 percent of the time.

The number of protons in the nucleus determines what element the atom is. The atom with eleven protons in its nucleus is sodium. The atom

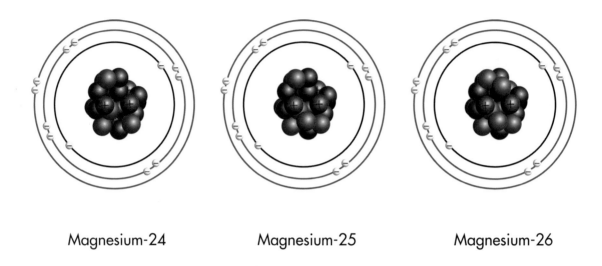

Magnesium-24   Magnesium-25   Magnesium-26

Magnesium occurs naturally in three isotopes. Magnesium-24, the most common, has twelve neutrons. Magnesium-25 has thirteen neutrons, and magnesium-26 has fourteen neutrons.

with thirteen protons in its nucleus is aluminum. Only the atom with twelve protons is magnesium.

With twelve electrons, elemental magnesium has three electron shells. The innermost shell is full, as is the second shell. The third shell, however, holds only two of a possible eighteen electrons.

The Role of Electrons

Electrons are much, much smaller than protons and neutrons. In fact, it takes 1,836 electrons to weigh as much as a single proton. If an electron weighed the same as a dime, a proton would weigh about as much as a gallon of milk!

Because electrons weigh so little, they don't really figure much into what's called the atomic mass (also known as atomic weight) of the atom, measured in atomic mass units (amu). The atomic weight is the average of the weights (or more accurately, masses) of all the different naturally occurring isotopes of an atom of a specific element. Magnesium's atomic mass is 24.3050 amu, which is sometimes rounded to two digits, 24, as it is in our periodic table (see pages 42–43).

Electrons do figure into the element's properties, though. That's because the number of electrons (and the number of empty spaces) in the outermost electron shell determines the reactivity of the element—for instance, how easily an element can form bonds with atoms of other elements to create the molecules of various compounds. These outermost electrons are called valence electrons.

The reason magnesium forms such stable compounds with other elements and burns so easily in oxygen, nitrogen, or carbon dioxide (because burning is really just an energetic chemical reaction to form new compounds) is that its outermost electron shell is nearly empty. Atoms are most stable when they have completely filled electron shells. Because magnesium has only two electrons in its outer shell, the easiest way for a magnesium atom to have a filled outer shell is to use those two electrons to form bonds with other atoms that are looking for electrons to fill their own outer shells.

There are two kinds of these bonds. In covalent bonds, atoms share electrons. In an ionic bond, one atom or group of atoms has donated one or more electrons to another atom or group of atoms. This leaves the electron donor atom with a positive charge, while the electon acceptor becomes negatively charged. An atom or group with an electrical charge is called an ion; hence the name, ionic bond. A cation is a positively charged ion, and an anion is a negatively charged ion. The electrostatic attraction of the oppositely charged ions is the basis for ionic bonding. When a magnesium atom donates its two valence electrons to another atom or group, it becomes a cation with a positive two charge. Magnesium's atomic structure is also what determines its place in the periodic table of elements.

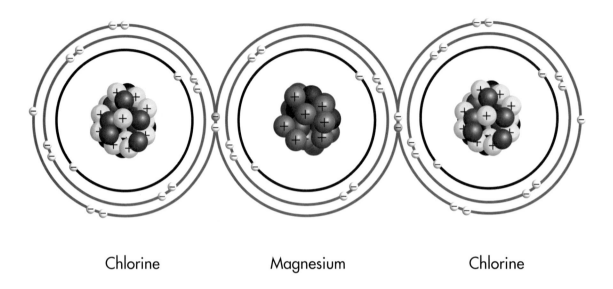

Chlorine   Magnesium   Chlorine

Magnesium shares one apiece of its two outermost electrons with two chlorine atoms to produce magnesium dichloride ($MgCl_2$), which is very stable because all the atoms have filled outer shells.

The Periodic Table of Elements

The periodic table began as a way to organize the elements for easier study. Scientists in the nineteenth century had noticed that if you arranged the elements by atomic mass, every eighth element had similar properties. Properties such as appearance and reactivity repeated periodically as the atomic mass increased. Hence the name, periodic table.

The father of the modern periodic table is generally considered to be Russian chemist Dmitry Mendeleyev. Beginning around 1871, his versions of the table listed the elements in rows by atomic weight, with the lightest element in each row on the left and the heaviest on the right, so that the elements with similar properties were stacked up on top of each other in columns. Sometimes placing known elements with similar properties

Magnesium Snapshot

Chemical Symbol:	Mg
Classification:	Alkaline earth metal
Properties:	Silvery-white metal, light, and strong; fine slivers or particles catch fire easily and burn with a brilliant white light
Isolated By:	Sir Humphry Davy
Atomic Number:	12
Atomic Weight:	24.3050 atomic mass units (amu)
Protons:	12
Electrons:	12
Neutrons:	12, 13, or 14 (for the three naturally occurring isotopes)
Density At 68°F (20°C):	1.74 grams per cubic centimeter (g/c^3)
Melting Point:	1,204°F (651°C)
Boiling Point:	1,994°F (1,090°C)
Commonly Found:	In magnesium compounds in the earth's crust (23,000 parts per million [ppm]); also present in seawater (1,200 ppm), soil (approximately 5 ppm), and the atmosphere (a trace)

in columns (or, to put it another way, avoiding placing elements with dissimilar properties in the same column) required leaving gaps in the table. By looking at the gaps, scientists could predict some of the properties of elements that hadn't yet been identified. When those elements were later identified and shown to fit into the gaps Mendeleyev had left, his version of the periodic table became widely accepted.

Of course, the periodic table has been greatly expanded and revised since Mendeleyev. For one thing, he knew of only seventy elements. Today, we know of ninety-two naturally occurring elements. Another three have been created by stars, and sixteen have been made artificially, bringing the current total to 111, with more waiting to be verified.

Periods and Groups

In the periodic table, the rows are called periods. Elements are arranged in the periods, left to right, in ascending order by atomic number. The atomic number is the number of protons in the nucleus of the element's atom. The atomic number determines an element's structure, properties, and place on the periodic table. In the case of magnesium, the atomic number is 12.

Each period represents the addition of one more electron shell. Hydrogen and helium, in period 1, have only one electron shell. The elements in period 2 have two; the elements in period 3, including magnesium, have three; and so on.

The columns or vertical arrangements of elements are called families or groups. Elements in a particular group have similar properties. Groups can be a bit confusing because there's more than one way to label them. The traditional method identifies two divisions, A and B, each of which has eight groups and are identified either by Roman numeral or Arabic numeral: VIIA or 7A, IIB or 2B, etc. However, the International Union of Pure and Applied Chemists, which sets standards for the naming of elements and the periodic table, now

	IA	IIA	IIIB	IVB	VB	VIB	VIIB	VIIIB	VIIIB
	1	2	3	4	5	6	7	8	9

Group →

Period										
1	1 1 **H** Hydrogen									
2	3 7 **Li** Lithium	4 9 **Be** Beryllium								
3	11 23 **Na** Sodium	12 24 **Mg** Magnesium								
4	19 39 **K** Potassium	20 40 **Ca** Calcium	21 45 **Sc** Scandium	22 48 **Ti** Titanium	23 51 **V** Vanadium	24 52 **Cr** Chromium	25 55 **Mn** Manganese	26 56 **Fe** Iron	27 59 **Co** Cobalt	Ni
5	37 85 **Rb** Rubidium	38 88 **Sr** Strontium	39 89 **Y** Yttrium	40 91 **Zr** Zirconium	41 93 **Nb** Niobium	42 96 **Mo** Molybdenum	43 98 **Tc** Technetium	44 101 **Ru** Ruthenium	45 103 **Rh** Rhodium	Pd
6	55 133 **Cs** Cesium	56 137 **Ba** Barium	57 139 **La** Lanthanum	72 178 **Hf** Hafnium	73 181 **Ta** Tantalum	74 184 **W** Tungsten	75 186 **Re** Rhenium	76 190 **Os** Osmium	77 192 **Ir** Iridium	Pt
7	87 223 **Fr** Francium	88 226 **Ra** Radium	89 227 **Ac** Actinium	104 261 **Rf** Rutherfordium	105 262 **Db** Dubnium	106 266 **Sg** Seaborgium	107 264 **Bh** Bohrium	108 277 **Hs** Hassium	109 268 **Mt** Meitnerium	

58 140 **Ce** Cerium	59 141 **Pr** Praseodymium	60 144 **Nd** Neodymium	61 145 **Pm** Promethium	62 150 **Sm** Samarium	63 152 **Eu** Europium	64 157 **Gd** Gadolinium	Tb
90 232 **Th** Thorium	91 231 **Pa** Protactinium	92 238 **U** Uranium	93 237 **Np** Neptunium	94 244 **Pu** Plutonium	95 243 **Am** Americium	96 247 **Cm** Curium	

A portion of the periodic table of the elements is pictured here. The alkaline earth metals, which include magnesium, form the second column (or group) from the left.

recommends that groups simply be numbered from 1 to 18. (See the periodic table on pages 42–43.)

Sometimes groups are referred to by the first element that appears at the top of the column: the beryllium (Be) group, the boron (B) group, the carbon (C) group, etc. Magnesium falls into group 2, the beryllium group.

There are also other common names for parts of groups, all of a group, or combinations of several groups. For example, there are the alkali metals (Li and down), the alkaline earth metals (Be family), the halogens (F and down), the noble gases (He family), and the transition metals (all the families from scandium, [Sc], through copper, [Cu], although sometimes the zinc [Zn] family is also included).

Magnesium is part of the alkaline earth metal group, along with beryllium (atomic number 4), calcium (atomic number 20), strontium (atomic number 38), barium (atomic number 56), and radium (Ra; atomic number 88). All of them have the same number of valence electrons—two—which gives them similar properties.

What's a Metal?

Magnesium is a metal. Metals are identified by the following four traits:

- Conductivity. Metals are good at conducting electricity. Silver (Ag), copper (Cu), and gold (Au), which are particularly conductive, are often used in electronic components for that reason. Magnesium conducts electricity, but it is only 39 percent as conductive as copper, and thus is seldom used as an electrical conductor.
- Reactivity. Most metals react easily with other elements and compounds to form compounds. Sodium and potassium are particularly reactive. Sodium, for example, reacts with water so enthusiastically that the hydrogen gas this reaction produces can burst into flames. Magnesium isn't as reactive as sodium or potassium, but it burns brightly in oxygen and will even burn in carbon dioxide or nitrogen.

Some examples of metals include copper (*lower left*), mercury (*upper center*), and magnesium (*lower right*).

- Ionic compound formation. Most metals, including magnesium, make positively charged ions by donating their electrons to other elements or groups of atoms.
- Alloyability. Metals can be easily mixed with other elements (often other metals) to make alloys, which have different properties from the component elements. Bronze, for instance, is an alloy of copper and tin that is stronger than either metal alone. Magnesium is frequently alloyed with aluminum. The aluminum improves magnesium's strength and corrosion resistance. It also makes it easier to weld.

   Some metals—gold, for instance—are sometimes found in nature in their pure form. Neither magnesium nor any of the other alkaline earth metals are found that way because they combine so readily with other elements to form compounds.

Chapter Three
How Magnesium Is Recovered

It's been said that when Sir Humphry Davy first isolated pure magnesium (and other elements) using electrolysis, he invented the entire light metals industry. That's because electrolysis continues to be the main method used to extract pure magnesium and other metals from the compounds in which they occur naturally.

In 1833, just twenty-five years after Davy first isolated magnesium, British physicist and chemist Michael Faraday passed an electrical current through dehydrated (water-free) molten magnesium chloride, producing liquid magnesium and chlorine (Cl_2) gas.

In 1852, Robert Bunsen, a German chemist most famous for the device named after him, the Bunsen burner, set up a small laboratory cell designed specifically for electrolyzing magnesium chloride. It was so successful that in 1886, the first commercial plant for producing magnesium was established in Hemelingen, Germany.

The first magnesium plant in the United States was constructed in 1914 in Schenectady, New York, by the General Electric Company. Magnesium production increased sharply during World War II because of magnesium's importance to the war effort, especially in the construction of incendiary bombs. In fact, the U.S. government constructed thirteen plants between 1940 and 1943 to supply magnesium for use in the war. Most of the plants were closed or sold to private industry after the war ended.

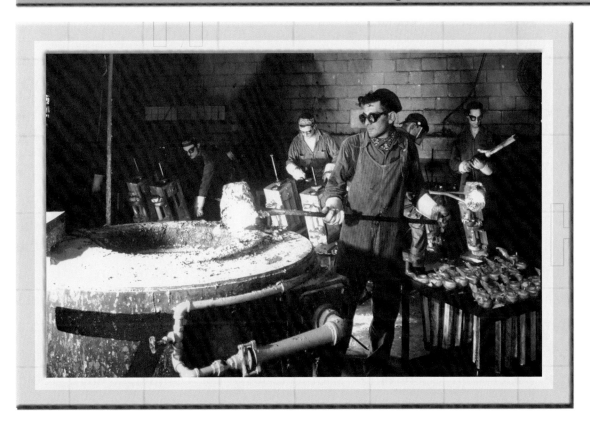

Workers in safety gear pour molten magnesium into casts to make bomb casings during the Second World War.

Today, the majority of the magnesium produced worldwide continues to come from the electrolysis of molten dehydrated magnesium chloride.

Making Magnesium

Before you can pass an electric current through molten dehydrated magnesium chloride, however, you have to produce dehydrated magnesium chloride (because water will react instead of the magnesium ion if it is present). One way to do that is to remove the water from magnesium chloride solutions. These are produced as by-products of the potassium industry or by dissolving magnesium-bearing minerals in hydrochloric acid (HCl). The magnesium chloride is mixed with an electrolyte, a substance that conducts electricity (typically one or a mixture of several compounds of potassium or sodium), at a temperature between 1,200° and 1,400° F (700° and 800° C). The mixture drives off the water in the container, which is either a brick-lined vessel or a steel shell. A powerful electrical current is passed through the mixture between two electrodes that are in separate compartments. The electrical energy simultaneously adds electrons to the magnesium cations to form magnesium metal and removes electrons from the chlorine anions from the magnesium chloride. The chlorine bubbles out of the mixture as a gas (Cl_2), and the magnesium floats to the surface in globules, since it's less dense than the electrolyte/magnesium chloride solution. The separate compartments are necessary because magnesium metal and chlorine gas react with each other spontaneously on contact, which would regenerate magnesium chloride.

There's a different method of producing magnesium used in a few locations. This method is the metallothermic reaction, and it's based on a different reaction: the reduction of magnesium oxide with ferrosilicon (FeSi).

The magnesium oxide comes from calcined dolomite, which is a mixture of magnesium oxide and calcium oxide (CaO). The metallothermic reaction to produce magnesium metal only happens under very high temperatures, between about 2,100° and 2,600° F (1,200° and 1,500° C). The reaction produces calcium silicate (Ca_2SiO_4) and iron metal, as well as magnesium metal.

It's estimated that more than 432,000 tons (392,000 tonnes) of magnesium are produced worldwide every year. That number is expected to exceed 1.1 million tons (1 million tonnes) by 2010. The top producers are China, Canada, and Russia. Traditionally, the United States is a top producer, but because its primary magnesium producer is a privately owned company, the production statistics are not publicly available.

Refining Magnesium

However the magnesium is produced, it must be refined to remove impurities. Refining involves melting the magnesium in large brick-lined furnaces or steel crucibles. A typical brick-lined furnace will hold anywhere from 10 to 25 tons (9 to 22.7 tonnes) of molten magnesium at once; the crucibles more typically hold 2 to 6 tons (1.8 to 5.5 tonnes). Most of the impurities in the magnesium are denser than pure magnesium, and thus settle out as sludge at the bottom of the furnace or crucible. Therefore, the pure magnesium can be simply poured off of the impurities.

Various additives can be put into the molten magnesium to help remove some substances. For instance, adding zinc chloride ($ZnCl_2$) or cobalt chloride ($CoCl_2$) can remove silicon. Stirring magnesium chloride into the melt can effectively remove elemental sodium and calcium by converting them into sodium chloride (NaCl) and calcium chloride ($CaCl_2$), which are denser than magnesium metal and therefore sink to the bottom.

The pure molten magnesium can then be cast into ingots or slabs. This process usually takes place in a special chamber where the air (which is made up mostly of oxygen [O_2] and nitrogen [N_2]) has been replaced by some other gas that is unreactive or inert toward magnesium so that it won't tarnish the magnesium. Magnesium ingots are sometimes coated with a thin layer of mineral oil for shipping to minimize the contact of the surface with air.

A lot of uses for magnesium require the metal to be in particles of various sizes and shapes. For example, very fine magnesium powder is used to add bright sparkles to fireworks. Larger particles are used when the metal is alloyed with other metals, like steel and aluminum, because the alloying process involves melting the metals together in large quantities to allow for mixing.

Particulate magnesium is produced from molten magnesium by shotting, atomization, or granulation. The process that is used depends on the size and shape of the particles desired. Shotting involves spraying molten magnesium into a cooling tower filled with an inert gas such as argon, helium, or methane (CH_4). The molten metal cools into tiny spheres 1/1,250 to 1/125 of an inch (0.2 to 2 mm) in diameter. Atomizing is also performed in a special chamber filled with an inert gas. Molten magnesium is sprayed onto a quickly rotating disk or into a fast-moving gas stream to make a fine powder. Granulation involves spinning molten magnesium in a rotating, perforated cup. As the cup spins, the metal exits through the holes in the side of the cup as fine granules that are the same size as the spheres produced by shotting.

Uses of Pure Magnesium

More than half of the magnesium produced is alloyed with about 10 percent aluminum, plus traces of zinc (Zn) and manganese. Mixing these metals in with magnesium improves magnesium's strength and resistance to corrosion, and makes it easier to weld. This alloy is used for automobile bodies and aircraft fuselages.

Another 20 percent of the magnesium produced is used in steel and iron production. Adding magnesium to the molten iron or steel removes sulfur, a contaminant that greatly weakens the metal.

The remainder is used in countless ways. For example, magnesium finds its way into hand tools, computers, lawn mowers, and digital cameras—to name just a few—to reduce weight. There are magnesium batteries used in sea-going safety equipment; these produce power once they're immersed in seawater.

Besides being used in the main bodies of automobiles and aircraft, magnesium is used for smaller pieces inside the vehicles, again, to reduce weight. Engineers are always looking for ways to reduce weight because, in both airplanes and automobiles, doing so reduces the amount of fuel the vehicle uses. A 10-percent reduction in the

Thanks to a shock- and vibration-resistant magnesium alloy body, this heavy-duty laptop computer can survive a 35-inch (90-cm) drop onto a steel plate.

weight of an automobile, for instance, translates into a 6- to 8-percent reduction in fuel usage. For that reason, magnesium is used in car parts as diverse as the instrument panel, the steering wheel, the outside mirror, and various brackets and clamps. Gearboxes, engine components, and even the engine block itself can be made from magnesium or magnesium alloys.

Pure magnesium has a number of important uses. However, as noted earlier, because of its reactivity, magnesium makes compounds with other elements very easily—and some of those compounds are just as important to us as pure magnesium itself.

Many magnesium compounds are minerals that contain magnesium in combination with many other substances. There are more than sixty magnesium-containing minerals. Among those, dolomite [$CaMg(CO_3)_2$], magnesite ($MgCO_3$), brucite [$Mg(OH)_2$], carnallite ($KMgCl_3 \bullet 6H_2O$) and olivine [$(MgFe)_2SiO_4$] all sometimes serve as the feed stock from which magnesium and magnesium compounds are extracted or manufactured. In the United States, magnesite and olivine are extracted from open-pit mines in the states of Washington, North Carolina, and Nevada.

Magnesium Oxide

Leading the pack of commercially important magnesium compounds is magnesium oxide, or magnesia. Magnesia is produced from magnesite, brucite, and dolomite, or extracted from seawater (which is about 0.13 percent magnesium). The iron and steel industries use vast quantities of magnesia in refractory linings to protect the inside of furnaces from the extreme heat of molten metal. (A refractory material is one that retains its strength even at extremely high temperatures.)

Magnesia is also used in farming as a fertilizer (see chapter 5 for more information about magnesium and its importance to green plants)

Extracting magnesium from seawater involves pumping the water into a settling pond like this one in the United Kingdom. As the water evaporates, dissolved minerals, including magnesium, are left behind.

and as an animal-feed supplement. Cattle and sheep that don't get enough magnesium in their diet can suffer from a potentially fatal disease called hypomagnesia, or grass tetany.

Magnesia is used as an ingredient in special cements that are used primarily as flooring in industrial buildings and as a stabilizing agent in rubber, among other things.

Magnesium Carbonate

Magnesium carbonate ($MgCO_3$), another important compound of magnesium, occurs naturally as magnesite, but the magnesium carbonate used in the United States is all synthetically manufactured. It's used in the pharmaceutical industry as an inert material: whenever you take a tablet, chances are, you're also taking magnesium carbonate. It's used as an inert binder to hold the actual particles of the drug together. It's also used in cosmetics, talcum powders, and the manufacture of soap because it can hold and carry a scent very effectively.

Magnesium carbonate is added to rubber and plastics as a flame retardant: it reduces the rate at which fire spreads and the amount of char and ash that is produced.

Magnesium Chloride

Magnesium chloride is recovered from brines—water that is heavily saturated with minerals, including table salt (NaCl) and magnesium chloride. In the United States, it comes from the Great Salt Lake in Utah. The already mineral-laden water from the lake is placed in shallow ponds and allowed to evaporate in the sun, concentrating it into brine, then processed further to separate the various salts in the brine, including magnesium chloride.

Magnesium chloride brine itself is used on dirt roads and construction sites and in mines and quarries to reduce dust. Magnesium chloride hexahydrate is sometimes used along with, or instead of, salt to spread on sidewalks and roads during the winter to melt ice or prevent ice from forming, especially if the surface is expensive to maintain. Magnesium chloride doesn't corrode asphalt or cement as much as salt does.

The Great Salt Lake

The Great Salt Lake is all that remains of Lake Bonneville, a huge lake that in prehistoric times was 1,000 feet (305 meters) deep. The Great Salt Lake, which varies significantly in size and depth depending on the weather, averages only 13 to 24 feet (4 to 7.3 m) in depth. At its largest (most recently, 2,500 square miles, or 6,477 square kilometers, in the mid-1980s), it's about 10 percent salt. That percentage increases when evaporation causes the lake to shrink.

Besides magnesium chloride, both potash [potassium carbonate] and table salt [sodium chloride] are extracted from brines created by allowing the salty water to evaporate. The only things that live in the lake's salty water are brine shrimp and certain kinds of algae.

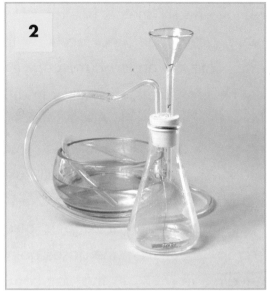

Magnesium reacts with hydrochloric acid to produce magnesium chloride and hydrogen gas: $Mg + 2\ HCl \cdot MgCl_2 + H_2$. A magnesium ribbon wrapped with copper wire (photo 1) is immersed in hydrochloric acid (HCl) (photo 2), in a flask that has a stopper (photo 3). Hydrogen gas bubbles into a water-filled container through a tube (photo 4).

Magnesium Hydroxide

Magnesium hydroxide [$Mg(OH)_2$] is also recovered from seawater or brines. It's used in industrial water treatment to reduce acid levels and remove heavy metals (metals not included in the alkali or alkaline earth metal groups and that occur in the lower regions of the periodic table; e.g., gold, silver, lead, mercury, etc.), which are particularly toxic.

Heavy metals can only remain dissolved in water that's fairly acidic. Reducing the acidity of the water makes most of the metal ions it contains insoluble as hydroxide (OH⁻) salts, causing them to precipitate out. Magnesium hydroxide, usually used in conjunction with sodium hydroxide (NaOH), also known as caustic soda, reduces the water's acidity.

Magnesium hydroxide is also used to reduce air pollution: it can "scrub" sulfur from the gases going up a power plant's chimney. The sulfur dioxide (SO_2) in the gas combines with the magnesium hydroxide, forming magnesium sulfite ($MgSO_3$) and water.

Magnesium hydroxide is used extensively in the manufacture of other magnesium chemicals and in some medicines, particularly antacid tablets and milk of magnesia (see chapter 5).

Magnesium Sulfate

Magnesium sulfate ($MgSO_4$), produced synthetically in the United States, is used in food additives (as a nutritional supplement providing extra

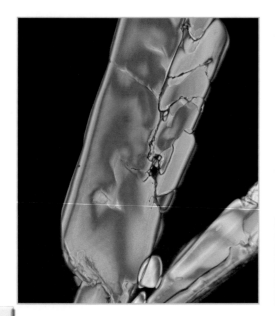

magnesium) and pharmaceuticals. One pharmaceutical use is in magnesium sulfate heptahydrate, known as Epsom salts. Many people find that soaking in a solution of Epsom salts reduces the pain of bruises, sprains, and insect bites.

This photograph shows a polarized light micrograph of magnesium sulfate ($MgSO_4$) that has crystallized out of a water solution.

Magnesium sulfate is also added to animal feed and is used in fertilizer for plants. A significant amount of the magnesium sulfate in the United States is used in the pulp and paper industry. In conjunction with sodium silicate ($Na_2O \bullet xSiO_2$), it extends the life of hydrogen peroxide (H_2O_2), which is a component in the bleaching process in some pulp mills.

Environmental Impact of Magnesium and Its Compounds

The ways magnesium and its compounds are used are practically endless, which raises the question: what are all those magnesium compounds used in industrial processes doing to the environment? The answer: not much. Magnesium and its compounds don't harm the environment because magnesium compounds naturally occur in relatively large amounts. The mining of magnesite and dolomite generally doesn't interfere with any other use of the land, and drainage from magnesite and dolomite mines doesn't contribute significantly to stream pollution. Processing the ore can be a dusty process, but dust collectors and wet scrubbers are able to control dust emissions.

Magnesium metal itself isn't harmful to the environment, but it can be hazardous to people because small pieces of magnesium, like dust or fine ribbons left over from shaping the metal, can react with water to generate hydrogen gas. This can be explosive if it builds up in a confined space. Therefore, these particles and slivers of magnesium are stored and shipped in special moisture-free containers, typically steel drums.

In magnesium plants, a chemical called sulfur hexafluoride (SF_6) is used to protect the molten magnesium from oxidation. The sulfur hexafluoride is thought to form a thin, protective film of magnesium fluoride (MgF_2) on the surface. There's concern that sulfur hexafluoride might be a particularly potent greenhouse gas—a gas that helps trap the sun's heat in the atmosphere, contributing to a warming of the planet. Researchers are currently seeking more environmentally friendly gases to replace it in magnesium production.

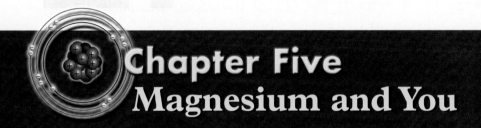

Chapter Five
Magnesium and You

Magnesium is more important to you than you probably realize, for the simple reason that without it, there would be no life on Earth, at least not as we know it. That's because magnesium is a crucial part of the chlorophyll molecule.

Chlorophyll is a type of molecule called a chelate. In chelates, a central metal ion is bonded to a large organic molecule at multiple sites. (An organic molecule is one composed of carbon, hydrogen, and other elements, like oxygen or nitrogen.) In chlorophyll, the central ion is magnesium.

Chlorophyll is essential to life on Earth because it is the green-colored substance that allows plants to use energy from the sun to turn carbon dioxide (from the atmosphere) and water into carbohydrates (food for the plant) and oxygen (which we then breathe).

When we eat plants, we get energy from the carbohydrates they contain, which they manufactured through the operation of chlorophyll. When we eat meat, we're eating proteins that were built by animal cells that received their energy from the carbohydrates the animals ate (or, in the case of carnivores, were eaten by the animals they, in turn, ate) in the form of green plants. In other words, the whole food chain depends on green plants, green plants depend on chlorophyll—and chlorophyll depends on magnesium.

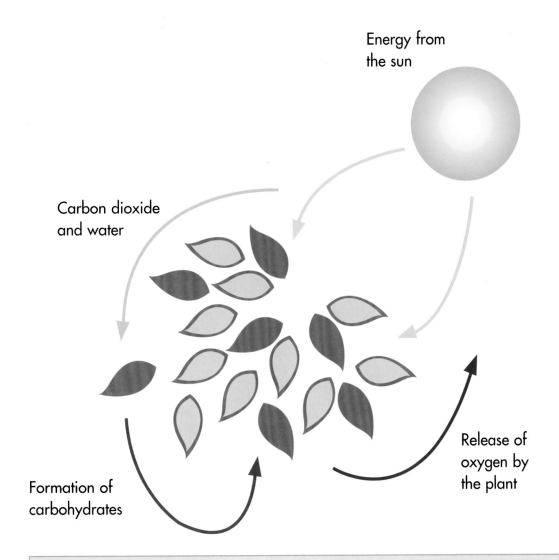

Energy from
the sun

Carbon dioxide
and water

Formation of
carbohydrates

Release of
oxygen by
the plant

> Magnesium is an essential element of chlorophyll, which enables plants to use energy from the sun to turn carbon dioxide and water into food (carbohydrates) and oxygen (which we breathe).

Magnesium in the Body

Even though you're not a green plant, you also use magnesium in your body. Plants get their magnesium from the soil (which is why magnesium salts are included in commercial fertilizers), and we get our magnesium from plants. On average, you need about 0.01 ounce (283 milligrams) of

This figure contains images of crystals of trace elements found in the human body. Iodine (red) and manganese (blue-brown) are at the head and neck level, magnesium is at the thigh level, and potassium is at the shin level.

magnesium every day. You probably take in about 350 milligrams (.012 ounce) just by eating a balanced diet.

About 60 percent of the magnesium in our body is used for our skeletons. It helps maintain bone structure. Furthermore, the bones act as a store of magnesium that the body can call on as required, so even if you don't get enough magnesium for a day or two, you're unlikely to run short.

In the rest of the body, magnesium serves several important functions. Magnesium ions help regulate the movement of substances through the body's membranes. They activate more than 100 of the important chemicals called enzymes that help the body's chemical reactions operate as quickly as we need them. They are used in building proteins and are involved in the replication of DNA (the material found in a cell's nucleus that determines the genetic traits of an organism).

Milk of Magnesia

Magnesium does have medical uses, but because magnesium deficiency is very rare, that's not usually what it's used for. Probably the best-known medicine containing magnesium is a sticky white liquid that looks a bit like milk, which is how it got its name: milk of magnesia.

Milk of magnesia does not contain any milk. It's simply a suspension of about 8 percent magnesium hydroxide in water. (A suspension is a mixture of a solid and a liquid in which the solid is not completely dissolved in the liquid and is instead present as solid particles.) Milk of magnesia is used primarily as a mild laxative. In the intestinal tract, milk of magnesia draws water from the surrounding tissue. This water softens the feces and increases its volume, both of which are likely to lead to a bowel movement.

Milk of magnesia is also used as an antacid. The hydroxide ions (OH^-) from the magnesium hydroxide combine with the hydrogen ions (H^+) in stomach acids to form water, thus neutralizing the acid. Magnesium oxide, magnesium carbonate, tribasic magnesium phosphate

Milk of magnesia, shown here, is used primarily as a mild laxative. It is about 8 percent magnesium hydroxide suspended in water.

$[Mg_3(PO_4)_2 \cdot 5H_2O]$, magnesium trisilicate $(2MgO \cdot 3SiO_2 \cdot nH_2O)$, and magnesium citrate (a compound of magnesium carbonate and citric acid) can also be used as antacids, and magnesium sulfate and magnesium citrate are also used as laxatives.

Magnesium compounds are used medically to relieve pain and reduce fever (magnesium acetylsalicylate $[MgCl_8H_{14}O_8]$, which is related to aspirin), to kill germs (magnesium borate $[BH_3MgO]$, magnesium salicylate $[MgC_{14}H_{10}O_6]$, and magnesium sulfate), and to help people sleep (magnesium bromide $[MgBr_2]$).

Magnesium stearate $(MgC_{36}H_{70}O_4)$, which acts as a lubricant, has a role in making pills—not as a substance in the pills, but as a way of preventing the pills from sticking to the equipment that is used to make them.

Get a Grip

There's one compound of magnesium you've probably seen many times without realizing it had anything to do with magnesium. Have you ever seen a weightlifter or gymnast rub his or her hands with a white powder before performing? That white powder is usually called chalk, but it isn't the same kind of chalk you write on a blackboard with. Instead, it's magnesium carbonate $(MgCO_3)$. It binds with any water on the athlete's

An athlete prepares his hands with chalk (magnesium carbonate) before competing in the shotput. The chalk binds with water, drying the athlete's hands.

hands, drying out his or her skin and ensuring a better grip on the barbell or gymnastic equipment.

There's another kind of chalk that is also a magnesium compound. It's what tailors use to mark clothing for alteration (welders and metal cutters use it, too). It's typically talc, or hydrated magnesium silicate [$Mg_3Si_4O_{10}(OH)_2$].

Powdered talc, or talcum powder, is used as a cosmetic powder and especially in baby powder. Baby powder's ability to absorb moisture makes it ideal for preventing diaper rash, which is caused by a wet diaper being in contact with an infant's sensitive skin over a long period of time. One of the very first things to touch your tender bottom after you were born was probably a magnesium compound. See how important magnesium is to you?

The Periodic Table of Elements

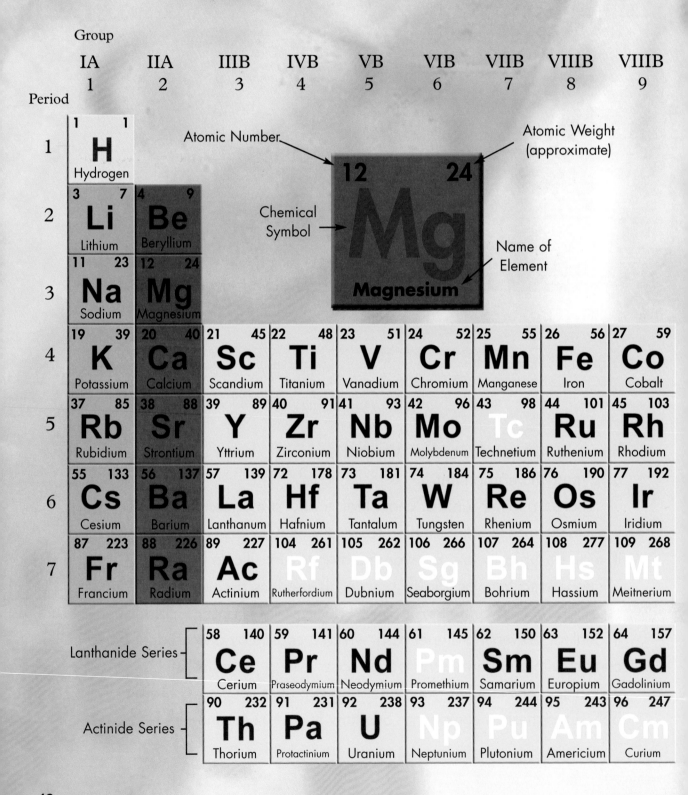

42

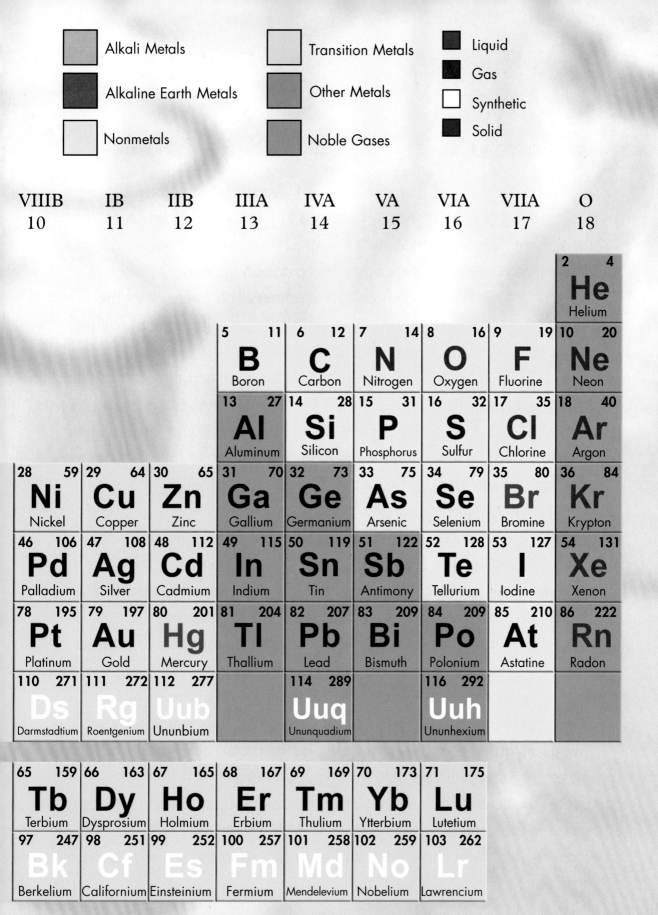

Glossary

alloy A mixture of two or more different elements, often metals.

atomic number The number of protons in the nucleus of an atom of an element. This also equals the number of electrons. The atomic number determines an element's properties and place on the periodic table.

atomic weight Also known as atomic mass. The average of the weights (or more accurately, masses) of all the different naturally occurring forms (isotopes) of an atom of a specific element.

compound Two or more atoms bound together into a molecule by the sharing of their atoms' electrons, or by the attraction of their ions.

electrolysis Passing an electrical current through a compound in order to cause a redox reaction (the addition of electrons to one substance and the removal of electrons from another substance).

electron A negatively charged particle.

element A substance made up of only one kind of atom.

group The elements in a column of the periodic table.

ion An atom or a molecule that has a positive or negative electrical charge from having acquired or lost one or more electrons.

isotope An atom of an element that has the same number of protons but a different number of neutrons.

molecule The smallest particle of a substance, consisting of two or more atoms that are bonded by the sharing of their electrons, and that exists on its own and still maintains its properties.

neutron A subatomic particle that has no charge.

nucleus The central portion of an atom, made up of protons and neutrons.

period In the periodic table, each row of elements.

proton A positively charged subatomic particle found in the nucleus of an atom.

International Magnesium Association
1000 N Rand Road, Suite 214
Wauconda, IL 60084
(847) 526-2010
Web site: http://www.intlmag.org/

International Union of Pure and Applied Chemistry
IUPAC Secretariat
P.O. Box 13757
Research Triangle Park, NC 27709-3757
(919) 485-8700
Web site: http://www.iupac.org

Thomas Jefferson National Accelerator Laboratory
Office of Science Education
628 Hofstadter Road, Suite 6
Newport News, VA 23606
(757) 269-7560
Web site: http://education.jlab.org/

Web Sites

Due to the changing nature of Internet links, Rosen Publishing has developed an online list of Web sites related to the subject of this book. This site is updated regularly. Please use this link to access the list:

http://www.rosenlinks.com/uept/magn

For Further Reading

Ball, Philip. *The Ingredients: A Guided Tour of the Elements.* New York, NY: Oxford University Press, 2002.

Emsley, John. *Nature's Building Blocks: An A–Z Guide to the Elements.* New York, NY: Oxford University Press, 2001.

Knapp, Brian. *Calcium and Magnesium.* Danbury, CT: Grolier Educational, 2002.

Newton, David E. *Chemical Elements: From Carbon to Krypton.* Detroit, MI: U•X•L, 1999.

Stwertka, Albert. *A Guide to the Elements.* 2nd ed. New York, NY: Oxford University Press, 2002.

Bibliography

Brown, Bob. "History of Magnesium Production." Magnesium.com. Retrieved June 2006 (http://www.magnesium.com/w3/data-bank/index.php?mgw=196).

Cole, Gerald D. "Magnesium." *Chemical and Engineering News.* Retrieved June 2006 (http://pubs.acs.org/cen/80th/magnesium.html).

"Humphry Davy." Chemical Achievers. Retrieved June 2006 (http://www.chemheritage.org/classroom/chemach/electrochem/davy.html).

"It's Elemental." Thomas Jefferson National Accelerator Laboratory Office of Science Education. Retrieved June 2006 (http://education.jlab.org/itselemental/index.html).

"Joseph Black, M.D." University of Glasgow Department of Chemistry. Retrieved June 2006 (http://www.chem.gla.ac.uk/dept/black.htm).

Kramer, Deborah A. "Magnesium, Its Alloys and Compounds." U.S. Geological Survey Open-File Report 01-341. Retrieved June 2006 (http://pubs.usgs.gov/of/2001/of01-341/).

"Physical Properties." International Magnesium Association. Retrieved June 2006 (http://www.intlmag.org/physical.aspx).

"Sir Humphry Davy." Woodrow Wilson National Fellowship Foundation. Retrieved June 2006 (http://www.woodrow.org/teachers/chemistry/institutes/1992/Davy.html)

Index

A

atom, defined, 14

B

Black, Joseph, 8–9
Bunsen, Robert, 24
Bussy, Antoine-Alexandre-Brutus, 11

C

chlorophyll, 5, 36

D

Davy, Humphry, 9–11, 24

E

electrolysis, 9–10, 24, 25

electrons, role of, 16–17
environment, impact of magnesium on, 35
Epsom salts, 4, 6–7, 34

F

Faraday, Michael, 24
flash bulbs/flashes, 13

G

Great Salt Lake, 32

I

isotopes, defined, 15

M

magnesium
in the body, 37–39

compounds of, 4, 5, 6–7, 8, 11, 17, 25, 26, 30–35, 39–41

as element, 4, 6, 11, 15–16, 17, 22

extracting/producing, 24, 25–26

isolation of, 8–9, 10–11, 24

isotopes of, 15

properties of, 11–13, 22–23

refining, 27–28

uses for, 4–5, 7, 13, 24, 27, 28–29, 30–31, 32, 33–35, 39–41

where it's found, 6

Mendeleyev, Dmitry, 18, 19

metallothermic reaction, 26

metals, described, 22–23

milk of magnesia, 39

P

periodic table of elements

creation of, 18–20

organization of, 20–22

R

Rupprecht, Anton, 9

S

subatomic particles, 14–15, 16

About the Author

Edward Willett vividly remembers the junior high science class where he saw magnesium burn for the first time. He's been interested in the metal, and its myriad uses, ever since. Today, Willett, the author of many books of nonfiction for children, writes a weekly science column for newspapers and radio. He resides in Regina, Saskatchewan.

Photo Credits

Cover, pp. 1, 15, 16, 18, 21, 37, 42–43 by Tahara Anderson; p. 5 © Astrid & Hanns-Frieder Michler/Photo Researchers, Inc.; p. 7 © G. Brad Lewis/Photo Researchers, Inc.; p. 10 © DK Limited/Corbis; pp. 12, 33 by Mark Golebiowski; p. 13 © Bettmann/Corbis; p. 23 © Andrew Lambert Photography/Photo Researchers, Inc.; p. 25 © Robert Yarnall Richie/Time Life Pictures/Getty Images; p. 29 © YOSHIKAZU TSUNO/AFP/Getty Images; p. 31 © Robert Brook/Photo Researchers, Inc.; p. 34 © Eye Science/Photo Researchers, Inc.; p. 38 © Alfred Pasieka/Photo Researchers, Inc.; p. 40 © David Frazier/Photo Researchers, Inc.; p. 41 © Mark Dadswell/Getty Images.

Special thanks to Jenny Ingber, high school chemistry teacher, Region 9 Schools, New York, New York, for her assistance in executing the science experiments illustrated in this book.

Designer: Tahara Anderson; Editor: Kathy Kuhtz Campbell